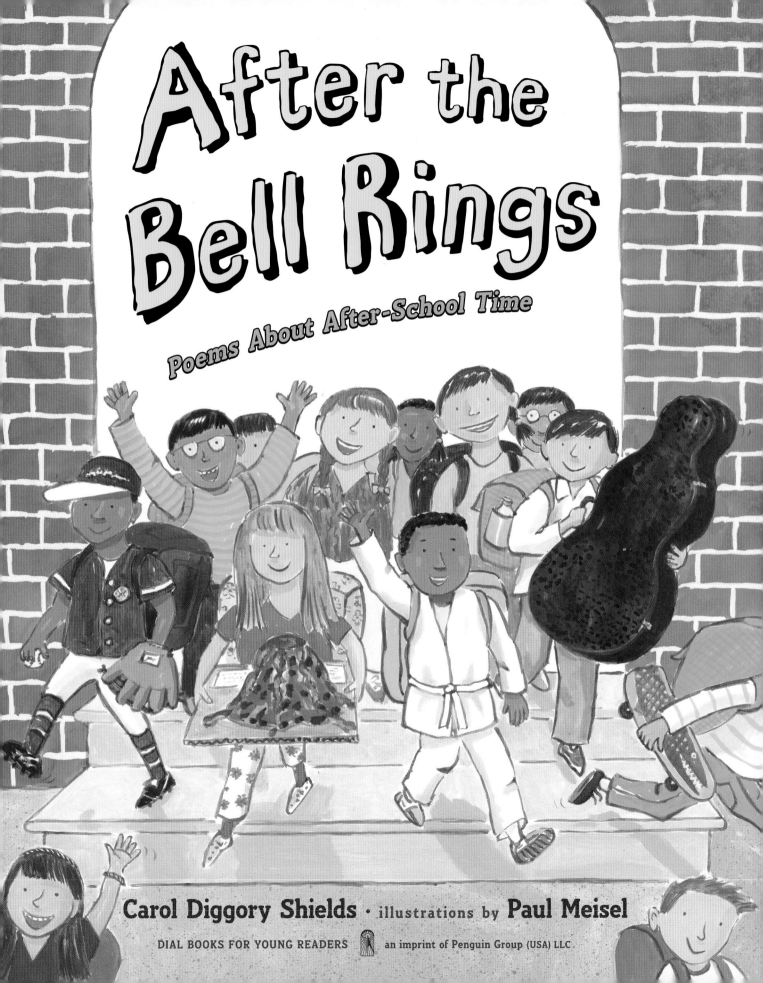

After the Bell Rings

Poems About After-School Time

Carol Diggory Shields · illustrations by **Paul Meisel**

DIAL BOOKS FOR YOUNG READERS · an imprint of Penguin Group (USA) LLC

For my very busy grandsons,
Sean and Grant, with love
—C.D.S.

For teachers and librarians,
who do the heavy lifting
—P.M.

DIAL BOOKS FOR YOUNG READERS
Published by the Penguin Group • Penguin Group (USA) LLC, 375 Hudson Street, New York, NY 10014

USA | Canada | UK | Ireland | Australia | New Zealand | India | South Africa | China
penguin.com

A PENGUIN RANDOM HOUSE COMPANY

Text copyright © 2015 by Carol Diggory Shields • Illustrations copyright © 2015 by Paul Meisel

Library of Congress Cataloging-in-Publication Data
Shields, Carol Diggory. • [Poems. Selections]
After the Bell Rings : Poems About After-School time / by Carol Diggory Shields ; pictures by Paul Meisel.
pages ; cm • ISBN 978-0-8037-3805-8 (hardcover : acid-free paper) 1. Children's poetry, American.
I. Meisel, Paul, illustrator. II. Title. • PS3569.H48328A6 2015   811'.54—dc23   2014002797

Manufactured in China on acid-free paper • 10 9 8 7 6 5 4 3 2 1

Designed by Jason Henry • Text set in Pueblo • The artwork for this book was executed on
140 pound Arches hot press paper using acrylic, gouache, and colored pencil.

CONTENTS

2:48

Like horses at the starting gate,
We shift and shuffle—we can't wait.
Our papers are stapled, our markers are topped,
But it feels like the clock on the wall has stopped.
The teacher is giving us all dirty looks,
As we softly, quietly close our books,
Hands folded on desks, we smile into space,
(With our feet we are nudging our backpacks in place).
Then finally, finally, *finally*, *BRRRRRIIIING!*
That wonderful bell begins to ring.
With polite good-byes we walk out, one by one,
Another school day, over and done!

2:48

2:48—this day's been fun,
But I'm kind of glad it's almost done,
Papers in my briefcase, pens in the drawer,
Soon after that bell I'll be out the door.
I'll text some friends, maybe ride my bike,
Have a snack, do whatever I like.
Still 2:48, says the clock on the wall—
These last 2 minutes are the slowest of all!

Level 5

My parents said, "No video games
Till all your homework's done."
But they weren't home and so I thought,
Well, I will just play *one*.
My score was really lousy,
So I had to play some more,
And then before I knew it,
I got to Level Four.
No way to stop—just two more points,
I'd get to Level Five!
When suddenly I heard Mom's car
Pulling in the drive.
I grabbed a book, put on a look
That said I could be trusted.
She put her hand on the warm TV,
"Guess what, kid? You're busted."

Hi, Mom!

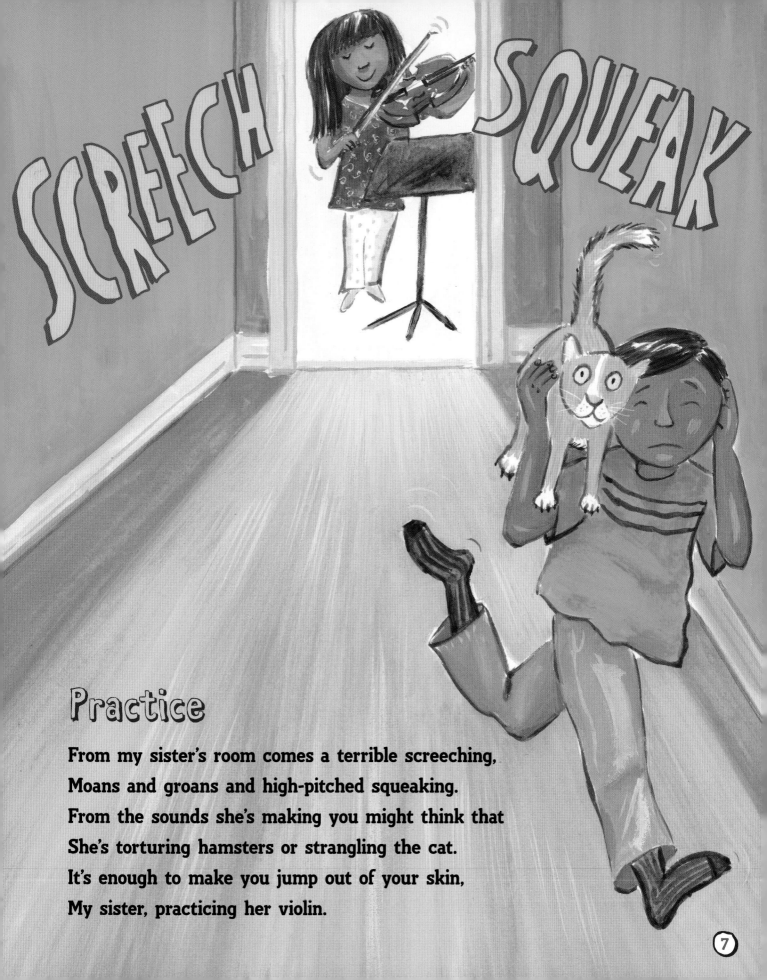

Practice

From my sister's room comes a terrible screeching,
Moans and groans and high-pitched squeaking.
From the sounds she's making you might think that
She's torturing hamsters or strangling the cat.
It's enough to make you jump out of your skin,
My sister, practicing her violin.

Homework #1

I have to write a poem,
But I'm having a hard time,
Getting stuck on words
That do not have a rhyme.
Of course there is that lonely orange,
Which doesn't have a mate.
Well *purple* doesn't either,
Just to set the record straight.
Circus, *film*, and *pizza*,
Can't rhyme them in a poem.
Laundry, *wolf*, and *ogre*,
Each one stands alone.
Monster, *penguin*, *office*, *silver*—
Not one has a match,
Nor *almond*, *olive*, *month*, or *scalp*,
(Which I begin to scratch).
Depth or *width* or *shadow*,
It just keeps getting worse!
I give up—the poem I write
Will have to be blank verse.

Escape

Out of the prison gates I slip,

I zig and zag, I dodge and dip,

Through the dark forest of towering trees,

Leaving no trail for my enemies.

Across the wild river on a narrow log,

Past the castle with the howling wolf-dog,

One last mad dash! I got home okay!

Good thing that my school is just three blocks away.

Snack Attack

I'm staring into the fridge,
Don't know what I will find . . .
I really want something to eat,
But my stomach can't make up its mind.

Does it feel like something fruity?
Spicy, tart, or gooey?
Salty, noodle-y, crispy,
Or something nutty and chewy?

Something creamy and sweet?
Or something covered with cheese?
I hope my stomach decides
Before I totally freeze.

Manga

Manga like really I
Cool it's think I
Rule stories the and graphics the
Tend I now is problem only the
.End the from book every reading start to

txt msgs

i h8 ths hmwrk

i do 2

mathz ez. spLN? no clu

itz 4eva snce i 8

watz 4 suppa?

pza

gr8!

i c u r almst dun

arrrrrgh. pencl broK. do u hav 1?

no prob. 4 sure I do

thnx. gld i m sittN nxt 2 u!

Booked

Monday: band
Tuesday: basketball
Wednesday: judo
Thursday: study hall
Friday: clarinet
Saturday: tap
When Sunday comes around,
I just want to take a nap.

Homework #2

I'd rather take the garbage out,
Eat a soggy Brussels sprout,
Clean the litter box of poo,
Than do the homework I must do.

I'd rather kiss Great-Aunt Irene,
Scrub the toilet nice and clean,
Chase spiders from the garden shed,
Than do the homework that I dread.

I'd rather change the baby's diaper,
Cuddle with a deadly viper,
Give our mean old cat a bath,
Than do the homework I hate—*math*.

Untitled

My shoulders are aching, my back's out of whack.
With every step, my knees pop and crack.
I shuffle my way to and from school,
Like an overburdened mule.
I used the scale, found out it's true—
My backpack weighs twice as much as I do.

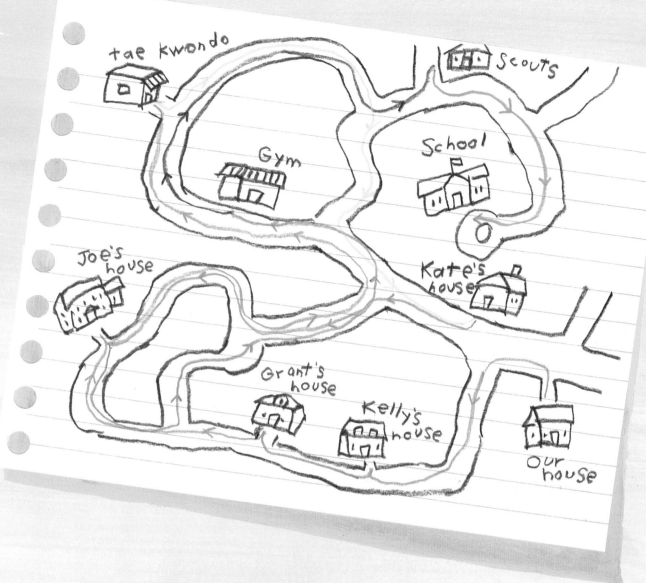

Car Pool

We pick up Kelly, Grant, and Joe,
Drop Molly off at tae kwon do,
Pick up Stef and Sam at Kate's,
Go back to Joe's (forgot his skates),
Leave Sam and Alex at the gym,
Take Sean to Scouts and pick up Kim,
Drop Dave at band so they can rehearse,
Then do it all over—this time in reverse.

Friday Night

We call it sleeping over—
That's not exactly true.
We bring along our sleeping bags,
But sleep? Not what we do.

We watch a scary movie,
Get all freaked out about it,
Shiver under blankets,
But sleep? I really doubt it.

We make snacks in the kitchen,
Using every pot,
Nachos, pizza, pudding, popcorn,
Sleeping? I think not.

We do our nails and faces,
Try out sprays and gloss and creams,
Invent some crazy hairstyles,
But sleeping? In your dreams!

Greetings !

When I get home from school at four,
He runs to greet me at the door,
Jumps up and down and yips with joy,
Then zips off to bring me a toy.
Gives me a great big doggy kiss,
To let me know that I was missed.

22

Greetings 2

When I walk up the driveway, he's suddenly there,
Strolling along with his tail in the air.
He darts out in front, then suddenly stops,
Drops to the ground, rolls and flip-flops.
Purrs loud as a train on a railroad track,
That's how a cat says, "I'm glad you are back!"

Contagious

Tonight I'm feeling dizzy,
My stomach's in a knot,
Don't get too close! Or you might catch
Whatever it is I've got.
My liver feels all achy,
(Or maybe it's my spleen).
It might be wise for me to spend
This week in quarantine.
I'd better stay home tomorrow
(Might be the plague, or swine flu!),
Though it's too bad—tomorrow's the day
My oral report is due.

Bored

You've finished all your homework,
You've had a snack or three,
Your buddies are all busy,
And there's nothing on TV.
Here's a little tip,
Just from me to you,
Never, ever say "I'm bored!
I've got nothing to do."
So quickly that your head will spin,
Your dad will have you mowing,
Digging, raking, hauling,
Stacking, sweeping, hoeing.
Your mom will have you sweeping,
Scrubbing garbage cans,
Washing, folding, polishing,
Or cleaning out the van.

You may be bored out of your gourd,
Look busy and don't show it.
And most importantly of all,
Don't let your parents know it!

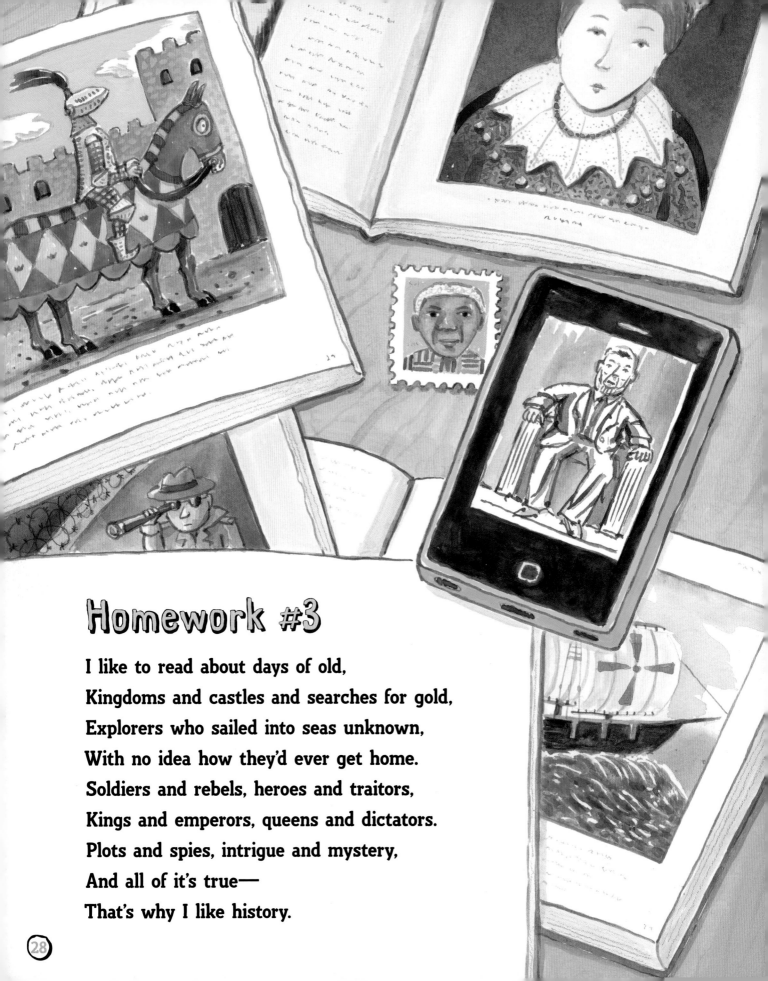

Homework #3

I like to read about days of old,
Kingdoms and castles and searches for gold,
Explorers who sailed into seas unknown,
With no idea how they'd ever get home.
Soldiers and rebels, heroes and traitors,
Kings and emperors, queens and dictators.
Plots and spies, intrigue and mystery,
And all of it's true—
That's why I like history.

Untitled

We've got a baby in our house.
I'd really rather have a mouse.
Mice are nice and they just squeak,
While babies howl and yowl and shriek.
After school my friends come round,
But hush! We cannot make a sound!
He's napping—can't do what we wanna.
I wish we had a pet piranha.
Can't use my room, because we share it,
Couldn't we just get a ferret?
"You'll have such fun, when he gets big,"
But I'd rather have a guinea pig.

Homework #4

I need a science project for school,
An experiment that is really cool.
Something that will awe and surprise,
(Maybe I'll win a Nobel Prize).
A project with wires and buzzers and bells,
Or bubbling beakers with horrible smells.
A project that will make me look like Einstein,
And one I can finish by bedtime, at nine.

Extracurricular

My favorite activity, after school,
Doesn't require a gym or a pool,
A diamond, a track, no goals or mats,
No helmets, shin guards, balls, or bats.
No cleats, no uniform to wear,
(I can do it in my underwear).
There's really nothing that I need—
Just a quiet spot and a book to read.